Hosea

31 Daily Insights from God's Word by **David Gibb**

Journey through Hosea
© 2015 by David Gibb
All rights reserved.

Discovery House is affiliated
with Our Daily Bread Ministries.

Requests for permission to quote
from this book should be directed to:
Permissions Department
Discovery House
P.O. Box 3566
Grand Rapids, MI 49501
Or contact us by email at
permissionsdept@dhp.org

This Discovery House edition is published with the permission of 10Publishing (UK), who previously published *Hosea: His Redeeming Love* and holds the publishing licence to the work. 10Publishing is a division of 10ofthose.com

Design by Joshua Tan
Typeset by Grace Goh

ISBN 978-1-9996690-6-5

Printed in the United Kingdom
First Printing in 2018

Foreword

"How are you feeling?" We are used to asking this question of each other, but have you ever stopped to ask it of God? Other books in the Bible tell us what God thinks, what He demands, and what He expects, but this book by the prophet Hosea shows us, in a way that few other parts of Holy Scripture do, just how God feels.

The book of Hosea is not a message from God coldly delivered by a detached onlooker. As God's spokesman, Hosea is told by Him to marry Gomer, a prostitute, and to go again and again to woo her back despite her many infidelities. It is, quite frankly, shocking! But that is precisely the point. For in Hosea's commitment to love Gomer we see a dim reflection of God's love for us. It is completely undeserved, and yet, astonishingly, even when we wander from Him and our hearts cool towards Him, He continues to come after us and to draw us back to Him. His love is one that will never let us go.

This is the Bible's very own love story. As you read through Hosea, my prayer is that you will fall in love with God all over again.

To God be the glory,
David Gibb

We're glad you've decided to join us on a journey into a deeper relationship with Jesus Christ!

For over 50 years, we have been known for our daily Bible reading notes, *Our Daily Bread*. Many readers enjoy the pithy, inspiring, and relevant articles that point them to God and the wisdom and promises of His unchanging Word.

Building on the foundation of *Our Daily Bread*, we have developed this devotional series to help believers spend time with God in His Word, book by book. We trust this daily meditation on God's Word will draw you into a closer relationship with Him through our Lord and Saviour, Jesus Christ.

How to use this resource

READ: This book is designed to be read alongside God's Word as you journey with Him. It offers explanatory notes to help you understand the Scriptures in fresh ways.

REFLECT: The questions are designed to help you respond to God and His Word, letting Him change you from the inside out.

RECORD: The space provided allows you to keep a diary of your journey as you record your thoughts and jot down your responses.

An Overview

The opening verse of the book tells us that Hosea ministered "during the reigns of Uzziah, Jotham, Ahaz and Hezekiah, kings of Judah, and during the reign of Jeroboam son of Jehoash king of Israel". This is from around 760 to 715 BC. Israel had been torn into two kingdoms, Israel and Judah. The northern kingdom of Israel (whom Hosea chiefly spoke to) is at peace and is prosperous, but the mighty Assyria in the east is a potential threat. As we read further, we discover that all is not right. The people have forgotten God and turned to Baal, a local fertility god who promised bumper harvests. God has sent Hosea to warn His people and to woo them back to Him.

More prominently than any other book in the Old Testament, Hosea shows us that God loves His people as passionately and as jealously as a devoted husband loves his wife. The prophet not only says this, but also lives it; he learns how God feels towards His unfaithful people through the tragedy of his own struggling marriage.

In the structure of this book, we can see parallels between Hosea's marriage to Gomer and God's marriage to His people:

The Structure of Hosea

1:1–3:5   Faithful husband, unfaithful wife

4:1–11:11   Faithful God, unfaithful people

11:12–14:9   Repentance and restoration

Key Verse:
The LORD said to me, "Go, show your love to your wife again, though she is loved by another man and is an adulteress. Love her as the Lord loves the Israelites, though they turn to other gods and love the sacred raisin cakes."
—Hosea 3:1

Day 1

Read Hosea 1:1–3

Like the other prophets, Hosea begins his book by telling us when he spoke God's Word to the nation (Hosea 1:1). The background to this book is found in 2 Kings 14–20. While this is a period of political stability and material prosperity, it is also a time of gross idolatry. The powerful Assyrian empire is also steadily expanding towards the borders of Israel.

By this stage, in the middle of the eighth century BC, the kingdom has been torn in two. Both Hosea and Amos begin their ministry to Israel, the northern kingdom, at about the same time.

Nothing can prepare you for the shock of verse 2. God commands Hosea to go and marry literally "a wife of whoredom", a prostitute. Can God really be saying this? Adultery was listed as a prohibition in the Ten Commandments. It was disgraceful and demanded God's judgement. Yet here is God's own messenger being told by Him to marry an immoral woman. Why?

Notice the reason—"for like an adulterous wife this land is guilty of unfaithfulness to the LORD" (v. 2). In other words, the pain that Hosea would feel as he tries to love a woman who is continually unfaithful is a picture of the pain God feels in trying to love a people who continually go after other "lovers" or gods.

Have you ever thought about how God feels towards you? We say a lot about what God thinks and what He says, but Hosea is going to show us God's feelings. God feels passionately about His people. When the New Testament talks about Christ purchasing the church to be His bride, it has a close parallel with the theme of Hosea. God loves us deeply, and every time we flirt with sin or replace God with something or someone else, we hurt the One we are bound to.

So, Hosea is a love story.

In obedience, Hosea marries Gomer (v. 3). He is called by God not just to deliver a message, but also to live that message out in his own family life. He will know the pain and heartache of loving but receiving no love in return.

May this story rekindle your love and commitment to the One who loves you.

Heavenly Father, as I read this love story, please rekindle my love for you and my commitment to you. In Christ, who loved and gave himself for me, amen.

What does it say about God's Word that Hosea not only has to deliver it, but also has to live it out in his own family life? What does this teach us about the gospel?

What important lesson does Hosea (and, through him, the nation) have to learn about God's relationship to His people? Why do we need to learn this too?

Day 2

Read Hosea 1:4–11

Footballer David Beckham called his daughter "Harper Seven", actress Gwyneth Paltrow called her daughter "Apple", and musician Frank Zappa named his daughter "Moon Unit". Yet none of these are as shocking as the names God now tells Hosea to give his children. With each name, we see how hurt God is by His people's spiritual adultery, and how He will ultimately take action.

Hosea's first son will be called "Jezreel" (Hosea 1:4), after the place where an entire royal house of Israel had been butchered (2 Kings 9:21–10:10). It is meant to shock and warn Israel about what God is going to do.

When Gomer conceives again and gives birth to a daughter (Hosea 1:6), the girl is to bear the terrible name "Lo-Ruhamah". It means "not loved", for that is how God feels about His people. Their sin has so hurt Him that He will no longer love or forgive them.

Most distressing of all is the last child's name (v. 8): "Lo-Ammi", which means "not my people". Yet God had said to Moses, "I will take you as my own people, and I will be your God" (Exodus 6:7). Could this really be the end?

It is dangerous to presume on God's love. Is this a danger for you?

Yet, just when all seems lost, God speaks again. God remembers His promise to Abraham (Hosea 1:10, see Genesis 15:5). The promise of a vast people is still on track. And His promise to King David (Hosea 1:11, see 2 Samuel 7) of a united people with one king is also on track.

"Great will be the day of Jezreel" (Hosea 1:11). Yes, Jezreel stands for bloody massacre, but the word also means "God sows". Therefore, "Jezreel" is both a warning of judgement and a promise of a future harvest.

Hosea didn't know how God would hold those two together, but God's Son would one day hang on a cross, and His anger and faithfulness would meet there. Jesus would be shown no mercy so that God could have a people who would be shown mercy.

Heavenly Father, thank you that because of Jesus I can be your child and know mercy, amen.

How do verses 10–11 become true for us in Jesus Christ? Look up 1 Peter 2:9–10 and marvel at God's faithfulness!

What did it cost God to call you "my loved one" (Hosea 2:1)? How should we respond to such love?

Why is adultery so terrible? Why do you think God uses the marriage of Hosea to communicate to His people? Thank God for loving us with a love that will not let us go.

Day 3

Read Hosea 2:1–13

Chapter 2 opens with God, like an aggrieved husband, at the court filing charges for divorce. He says, "Rebuke your mother, rebuke her, for she is not my wife, and I am not her husband" (Hosea 2:2).

Why is He so angry? We see how far things have deteriorated between God and His people in verses 3–4. Note how strongly God feels and speaks. This is no small thing.

Yet look at what Israel said: "I will go after my lovers, who give me my food and my water, my wool and my linen, my oil and my drink" (v. 5). She thought she had got all she had by her cleverness in pursuing other gods (like Baal), but in verses 9–13 God says, "That's where you're wrong!" These things weren't Israel's but God's. He had given them the prosperity that they now enjoyed out of His love, and He could just as easily take it away.

God laments, "She has not acknowledged that I was the one who gave her the grain, the new wine and oil, who lavished on her the silver and gold—which they used for Baal" (v. 8). Can you hear the pain as God speaks? Like a husband who has given a keepsake to his wife only to discover that she has given it to another man, God feels cheated by His people, who had turned to foreign gods. No wonder He cannot bring himself to speak directly to His wife (vv. 2–4).

God had gone to great lengths to rescue His people, protect them, and provide for them. Under King Jeroboam II, they had become very rich. Yet Israel "decked herself with rings and jewellery, and went after her lovers", forgetting the Lord (v. 13). That's the danger of material prosperity. Moses had warned of this in Deuteronomy 8:10–14, 18–19. **When we enjoy material comforts, it's easy to think that we're in control and that we don't need God anymore.**

So God issues His people a final warning in verses 2–3. Essentially, He says: "Stop being unfaithful or I will take everything from you." It is a stark warning that we ignore at our peril.

Heavenly Father, show me where in my life I have forgotten you. Help me to turn from that attitude. In your mercy, amen.

Notice the language in verses 8 and 13. How does God feel about spiritual adultery?

In what areas might you be in danger of taking for granted what God has given you? What can you do so that you don't forget God?

Day 4

Read Hosea 2:14–23

What would you expect God to say after all the punishments He has promised to deliver in verses 1–13? "I will now destroy you utterly"? "I will wipe you off the face of the earth"?

No, that's not what He says. We read about God's ultimate intentions in verses 14–15: "Therefore I am now going to allure her; I will lead her into the desert and speak tenderly to her. There I will give her back her vineyards, and will make the Valley of Achor a door of hope."

How astonishing! Yes, Israel will be stripped naked (Hosea 2:3) and she will go back into the desert, but notice how tender this scene is.

"Achor" means trouble. **God will turn the valley of trouble into a door of hope.** Israel will look back on all the troubles God is about to bring on her and will say, "Though it hurt me, it was good for me, because it led me back to Him."

The desert experience will be hard, but it could be an opportunity too. Verses 6–23 tell us what God intends to do there. It will lead to:

• Frustration in pursuing idols (vv. 6–7). Like the prodigal son (Luke 15:16–17) who remembered home only when his stomach was empty, Israel will eventually return to God. What does it say about God's character that He will take us back even when our motivation is purely self-centred?

• A new devotion, as God's people discover that unlike the idols, God is not a vengeful master but a loving husband (v. 16).

• A new harmony, as peace between God and His people ripples forth (v. 18).

• A new vow, as God comes laden with betrothal gifts (v. 19).

• A new relationship with God that comes from knowing and obeying Him (v. 20).

• A new prosperity (vv. 21–22).

• A complete restoration of Israel as the bride of God (v. 23).

Would you have guessed that a chapter that began as this does, would end this way? What does this tell you about God?

Lord God, I know that sometimes you allow me to experience trouble and even lose things in order to bring me back to you. Help me to see this trouble as a door of hope. For Christ's sake, amen.

Did God have to take things away from you to bring you back to himself? Has God ever led you in and through trouble? Why was this good for you? (Read Hebrews 12:4–11 to find out why God sometimes disciplines us.)

Read through the chapter again and pray through the verses. What do you learn about yourself from these verses? What do you learn about God? What might God be wanting you to do as a result of this passage?

Day 5

Read Hosea 3:1–2

Marriages are easy to break; mending them is difficult, especially when adultery is involved. Chapter 3 tells the story of how Hosea has to learn to love his wife again, despite her unfaithfulness.

Hosea is told by God to "Go, show your love to your wife again, though she is loved by another and is an adulteress" (Hosea 3:1). Notice that:

- Hosea is to "go". He must take the initiative and make the first move, even though he is the wronged party.

- Hosea is to go "again". Despite Gomer's infidelities and constant extramarital affairs, Hosea must persist in his love towards her. God literally says, "Love your wife"; it is a command. Perhaps by this stage Hosea no longer feels any love for her, but reconciling love is a love that goes again and again, in spite of feelings.

- Hosea is to love Gomer even though she doesn't love him. Look at the second part of verse 1: "Love her as the LORD loves the Israelites, though they turn to other gods and love the sacred raisin cakes". God knows they don't love Him. He knows they prefer the other gods and the little delicacies (the raisin cakes) they eat at the festivals to Baal.

Moreover, Hosea has to buy his own wife back. "So I bought her for fifteen shekels of silver and about a homer and a lethek of barley" (Hosea 2:2). It looks like Gomer had run up debts and was forced to sell herself into slavery. Hosea swallows his injured pride, pays the debts, and opens his arms to Gomer again. Love pays the price.

Hosea's love for Gomer is a reflection of God's astonishing love for you and me. God has taken the initiative to seek out and save us. He offers forgiveness despite our unfaithfulness, and He paid a huge cost to redeem us even though He knows how fickle our love for Him is.

The apostle Peter writes: "For you know that it was not with perishable things such as silver or gold that you were redeemed from the empty way of life handed down to you from your ancestors, but with the precious blood of Christ, a lamb without blemish or defect" (1 Peter 1:18–19). God knows forgiveness is never cheap. If He is ever to have us as His people, He has to pay the price. Thank God, He has.

Thank you, dear Father, that we were not redeemed with perishable things such as silver and gold, but with the precious blood of Christ. Help us to see that cost and to be ever thankful, amen.

What "gods" (God-substitutes or "saviours") are you prone to turn to? Why? What is appealing about them? How do they compare to God and His love?

Look up 1 Peter 1:18–19. What comparison is being made here? Why? What value do you place on the blood of Christ? Knowing this, what should your attitude be towards Christ, as opposed to the "gods" you often turn to?

Day 6

Read Hosea 3:3–5

Our world is obsessed with quick answers: instant coffee, instant photography, instant messaging. But some things cannot be fixed in an instant. Hosea's marriage is one of them. It will take time and patience to heal.

Hosea understands that. Hence he tells Gomer, "You are to live with me for many days; you must not be a prostitute or be intimate with any man, and I will behave the same way towards you" (Hosea 3:3).

As the prophet opens his arms to Gomer again, he tells her not to play around anymore, or to be intimate with any man. And he adds, "I will behave the same way towards you", or literally, "I will wait for you". He will wait to be intimate with her again. He will make love to her when she is really committed to him, and not before. That will require real patience.

That's an important lesson for us who live in a time when so few people are willing to wait to have sex. Hosea is showing us that it takes time to grow to love someone deeply. God's purpose is that sex should be the consummation of that intimacy, not a shortcut to it.

Hosea begins to understand that God exercises patience with His people

too. Look at verses 4–5: "For the Israelites will live many days without king or prince, without sacrifice or sacred stones, without ephod or household gods. Afterwards the Israelites will return and seek the LORD their God and David their king. They will come trembling to the LORD and to his blessings in the last days."

Hosea sees dark days ahead for Israel: the monarchy and her religious life will fall. She will have nothing for a long time. But one day, in the last days, a new people of God will arise—a people who will be repentant and reverent, seeking to know God and His blessings, and submitting themselves once again to the kingship of David.

Thank God that He did not wash his hands of the human race. He will wait for us to return. **He is a God of extraordinary patience. Is He still waiting for you?**

Lord God, thank you for not washing your hands of us. Thank you for waiting for me to return to you. Help me to stay with you. In Christ's name, amen.

The words "live with" (Hosea 3:3) can also be translated as "wait for". What do we learn about God from Hosea's restraint?

How do the promises of verses 4–5 come true for us now (in part) and in the future (fully)?

How intimately do you know Christ? How might you get to know Him better?

Read Hosea 4:1–10

The story of Hosea's marriage now gives way to the second part of the prophecy: the even more heart-breaking account of Israel's unfaithfulness to the Lord (Hosea 4:1–11:11). In chapter 4 we begin to see just how far this adultery has spread.

The scene opens with God taking His people to court. His accusation is that "there is no faithfulness, no love, no acknowledgment of God" (Hosea 4:1), and the crimes He lists are straight from the Ten Commandments. **Rejecting God does not lead to a more moral society; it is always the reverse. Spiritual decay spawns moral decay.**

Spiritual decay also leads to environmental decay (v. 3). God had said, "If you defile the land, it will vomit you out as it vomited out the nations that were before you" (Leviticus 18:28). As with the land, so it was with the wildlife: birds and sea animals were all dying—nature itself was echoing Hosea's preaching. Rejecting God does not lead to life, but to death.

What about the religious leaders? Look at verses 4–5. God says, "My people are destroyed from lack of knowledge" (Hosea 4:6). Why is this so?

Firstly, the priests "have ignored the law of your God" (v. 6). Their job was to teach God's law to the people, but they had stopped doing that. Hence the nation was completely unaware of what it meant to know and follow God.

Secondly, the priests "feed on the sins of my people and relish their wickedness" (v. 8). They encouraged sin. As Hosea says in verse 7, "they exchanged their glorious God for something disgraceful". God was supposed to be their glorious God, but the priests encouraged idol worship instead, and were doing a roaring trade out of it. No wonder the Bible colleges were full! But looks can be deceptive, for "the more priests there were, the more they sinned against [God]" (v. 7).

What will God do? "It will be: like people, like priests. I will punish both of them for their ways and repay them for their deeds" (v. 9).

Each step in Israel's decline can be traced back to verse 1. So pray for yourself: pray for faithfulness, for love for God, and for true knowledge. Pray also for good church leaders.

Heavenly Father, please may I be faithful, love you, and know you today. May my church leaders not ignore your Word or encourage sin. In Christ's name, amen.

What is the link
between morality
(v. 2) and loving
and knowing God
(v. 1)? Why does our
society need to
know this?

What are the wider
consequences of
abandoning
God (v. 3)?

Why does God hold
the priests particu-
larly responsible
(vv. 4–10)? What
warnings are there
for church leaders?
What can you do to
try and ensure that
the church has good
leaders and not
bad ones?

Day 8

Read Hosea 4:11–19

God has had enough. In this figurative court of law, He is exposing Israel's crimes. Hosea now presents evidence for Israel's unfaithfulness. Some scholars and Bible translators believe that the section comprising verses 11–14 begins and ends with proverbs about Israel's lack of understanding. Sandwiched in between are the things that have made her foolish: drunkenness (Hosea 4:11), consulting idols for guidance (v. 12), and offering sacrifices at the hilltop pagan shrines (v. 13).

The men went up to these "shady" places (v. 13) to worship Baal by having sex with a shrine prostitute. It was supposed to encourage Baal to make the crops grow. Was it any wonder that the younger generation was turning to sexual immorality?

But notice how God will not punish the women for their lifestyle (v. 14), nor the wives for their affairs; it is the men He will hold responsible. They thought they could indulge in their drunken orgies without suffering the consequences, but all around them were the sad results of unfaithfulness and instability in their children's marriages.

Hosea directs his attention to Israel's sister nation, Judah. In essence, he gives Judah three warnings: "Watch out, Judah, that you don't catch Israel's idolatry and immorality, or you'll be next in the dock!" (v. 15, paraphrased).

"Watch out for Israel's religion!" (v. 15, paraphrased). Gilgal and Bethel were two of Israel's shrines. But "Bethel" (which means "house of God") has now become "Beth Aven" ("house of evil"). God warns Judah to keep away from such places of worship. Even Israel's liturgy had become corrupt—now they couldn't even say "As surely as the Lord lives" without it sounding like a chant to Baal.

"Watch out for Israel's obstinacy!" (v. 16, paraphrased). God longs to be a shepherd to Israel, but like a stubborn bull she won't budge. Tragically, for the people of Israel and those like them, there can be only one result—"a whirlwind will sweep them away, and their sacrifices will bring them shame" (v. 19).

What a warning! **God is love, but He is not soft. If we resist God and dig our heels in, it will not end well.** "A people without understanding will come to ruin" (v. 14).

Heavenly Father, help me to have true understanding, and so live to please you. In the name of Christ, amen.

Why does God hold the men responsible, rather than the immoral women? What lessons are there for us here?

What is Israel likened to (v. 16) and why? Why might God say the same of us?

Why is it important that we hold on to both pictures of God, as a lover in chapters 1–3, and as a judge in chapter 4?

Day 9

Read Hosea 5:1–7

The word "sorry" is one of the hardest words to say. Imagine someone deserting his or her spouse for someone else, then returning home. The marriage will never recover unless the errant spouse learns to say "sorry" genuinely from the heart. Hosea knew what it was like to wait for his wife Gomer's apology, and God knew it too as He waited to hear that word from the lips of His bride Israel.

Chapter 5 is all about a God who will exercise astonishing patience as He waits for that moment (Hosea 5:15). In verses 1–7 we see God taking the first step to get His people to that point.

Verse 6 tells us how God will deliberately withdraw himself from Israel. He knows that sometimes, the best way to deal with stubborn sinners is to let them feel the emptiness and loneliness of a world without Him. They may beseech Him with their sacrifices, but they won't find Him.

Why? Look at verse 1: "Hear this, you priests! Pay attention, you Israelites! Listen, royal house! This judgement is against you." God is saying: "It's no good for you priests to blame the kings, and the kings to blame the people. You are *all* to be blamed!"

The shrines at Mizpah and Tabor had become traps to get everyone to worship Baal. Israel wasn't fooling God, for He could read her like a book (v. 3). Their dabbling in sin now meant that they were unable to repent of their own will—the nature of sin did not permit them to even consider doing so (v. 4). It had paralysed them so that they couldn't return to God; it had perverted and captured their hearts (v. 4); and it had puffed them up (v. 5) with the illusion of being in control.

So, God will withdraw from them (v. 6).

Is that your experience? **Does God seem distant? He might just be waiting for you to say "I'm sorry" from the heart.**

Heavenly Father, give to me today a contrite heart that grieves over my sin and which seeks your forgiveness, genuinely. In the name of Christ, amen.

How does Proverbs
3:11–12 help us to
understand why
God sometimes
disciplines us?

What prevents
the people from
returning to God
(vv. 4–5)? How might
this happen? Can
you think of times
when you have been
unable to return
to God? What was
happening? How
should we view sin?

Why does God
choose to withdraw
from His people
(v. 6)?

Read Hosea 5:8–14

God is patiently waiting for His people to return to Him. He has told them that He is going to withdraw His affection (Hosea 5:1–7), and now He shows us the second step in His strategy to cause the Israelites to come to Him: He will apply discipline.

Verses 8–9 describe a military crisis. Assyria, under Tiglath Pileser III, was on the march. By then, Menahem was ruling Israel. He decided to pay Assyria a large tribute of silver to withdraw. This is probably what verse 13 means: "When Ephraim* saw his sickness, and Judah his sores, then Ephraim turned to Assyria, and sent to the great king for help."

Eventually, Pekah seized the throne and became king of Israel. Fearing another Assyrian attack, he persuaded the king of Damascus to side with him, and also tried to get King Ahaz of Judah to join them. But when Ahaz refused, Pekah invaded Judah and besieged Jerusalem. That drove Judah to seek Assyrian help, and Tiglath Pileser III duly invaded Israel and conquered much of her territory. A decade later, under Hoshea, Israel tried to regain her independence. This time, the Assyrians retaliated by completely destroying the kingdom and deporting the survivors; Israel was no more.

What does God say about all this? Read verses 13–14. God is saying:

"When Assyria pounces on Israel like a lion and when calamities descend on Judah, know that it is *I* who is coming against you!" Sometimes, God will allow us to reap the consequences of what we have sown. At other times, He will actively intervene and come against us. Why? Remember verse 15: He is waiting for His people to admit their guilt and seek after Him earnestly.

But "when Ephraim saw his sickness, and Judah his sores", what did they do? "Ephraim turned to Assyria, and sent to the great king for help" (v. 13). How hard it is for us to say sorry to God! It's much easier to devise some man-made answer to our problems. In Israel's case, she turns to Assyria rather than face up to God and seek His forgiveness.

It is wise to be humble and say sorry to God when we get things wrong.

Heavenly Father, please help me not to become proud, but to keep coming to you for forgiveness. Through Christ, my Lord, amen.

*Prophets used the terms "Ephraim" and "Israel" interchangeably when they spoke of the northern kingdom of Israel.

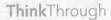

ThinkThrough

What does God promise to do to Israel (vv. 8–14)? Look at the images used and the use of "I will". What could prevent Israel from seeing these events as God's corrective discipline?

How did Israel respond (v. 13)? What does that reveal about us? What might God be revealing to you about himself and about your own character?

Day 11

Read Hosea 5:15–6:3

God is longing for His people to return to Him with penitent hearts. Verse 15 tells us why He will withdraw His affection from Israel (Hosea 5:1–7) and send Assyria to wound them (vv. 8–14): "I will return to my lair until they have borne their guilt and seek my face—in their misery they will earnestly seek me." Sometimes, it is only when we've been brought really low that we will truly seek after God, and that is what God waits for.

Yet it is possible to say "sorry" without meaning it. Scholars debate the meaning of Hosea 6:1–3. Is Israel going through the motions of repentance? Verse 2 seems to suggest that the Israelites believe that if they are sorry for "two days" or three, God will be merciful. Or are they truly penitent? Verse 3 suggests they intend to "press on". Whichever is true, the sort of confession God is looking for becomes apparent.

Firstly, God is looking for a frank confession of failure. They must admit their guilt (5:15). No more passing the buck.

Secondly, God is looking for a sincere turning of the heart towards Him. "They will earnestly seek me" (5:15). No more half-hearted prayers.

Lastly, God is looking for a humble confidence in His mercy. "He has torn us to pieces but he will heal us; he has injured us but he will bind up our wounds . . . he will restore us, that we may live in his presence" (6:1–2).

This is the sort of apology God waits to hear. When did He last hear it from you?

We need not doubt God's forgiveness when we offer such a confession of sin. Notice in verses 1–3 how often Hosea says "He will". To people who are genuinely sorry, God will grant to them a spiritual resurrection that lifts them out of the grip of sin: "After two days he will revive us; on the third day he will restore us, that we may live in his presence" (6:2).

Every one of us, even the most devoted, will sin. **Every one of us needs to say sorry, and to know His reviving, life-giving Spirit within us.** So turn to the Lord now, and sincerely confess your sin to Him.

Lord, have mercy. Christ, have mercy. Lord, have mercy, amen.

What does God say
He will do to bring
us back to himself
(Hosea 5:15)? What
does that tell you
about God?

Look at the sort
of apology God
longs for in Hosea
5:15–6:3. What is the
difference between
going through
the motions and
genuine repentance?
How can you avoid
the former and
embrace the latter?
Is there any area
in your life where
you are refusing to
acknowledge the
Lord?

Day 12

Read Hosea 6:4–6

Everyone experiences disappointment, from the student who studies hard but fails the exam, to the family who saves diligently to go on a dream holiday but suffers bad weather throughout the entire stay.

God knows disappointment too. After Israel's apology (Hosea 6:1–3), God now speaks of the frustration He feels towards Israel in verse 4: "What can I do with you, Ephraim? What can I do with you, Judah?" Parents would understand this feeling. There might be times we have said of our children, "I don't know what to do with them!"

This section of Hosea (6:4–7:16) describes God's disappointment with His children. Our scriptural passage for today shows us that God is disappointed with the emptiness of Israel's worship. Notice three elements:

Firstly, she blows hot and cold. "Your love is like the morning mist, like the early dew that disappears" (v. 4). Israel would acknowledge the Lord one minute and mean what she said at the time, but quickly forget her commitment. She would go through the phase of loving God, but it never lasted.

Secondly, she refuses to be taught. "Therefore I cut you in pieces with my prophets, I killed you with the words of my mouth—then my judgements go forth like the sun" (v. 5). God repeatedly rebuked the Israelites through His prophets' words and judgements (see 1 Kings 18:21, 38–40), and Israel would be devoted to God for a while, but turn back to idolatry again.

Thirdly, she goes through the motions. "I desire mercy, not sacrifice, and acknowledgment of God rather than burnt offerings" (Hosea 6:6). The Israelites would offer sacrifices as the law demanded, thinking that God would be on their side, but He was looking for something more. Hosea keeps using the words "mercy" and "knowledge" to speak of love and commitment. **God is looking for a personal relationship that lasts 24 hours a day, 7 days a week.** Centuries later, Jesus quoted this same verse to the Pharisees and said, "Go and learn what this means" (Matthew 9:13).

No wonder God was disappointed with Israel. How well do these verses describe your worship of God?

Heavenly Father, I confess that so often my worship of you is superficial. I need your Spirit to change my heart. Have mercy on me, for Christ's sake, amen.

In what ways
does your love
for God blow hot
and cold, like
Israel's? What other
"loves" capture
your attention and
affections? Ask
God to give you
an increasingly
undivided heart.

How teachable are
you? To what extent
are you prone to
going through the
motions in public
and private worship?
Pray that God will
help you to have
genuine love and
commitment.

Day 13

Read Hosea 6:7–7:7

You can't help feeling God's frustration with His people in the first verse of Hosea 7: "whenever I would heal Israel, the sins of Ephraim are exposed and the crimes of Samaria revealed". It is as though God is saying: "Whenever I try to show love to you, you go and sin again!"

If the problem in Hosea 6:4–6 was the emptiness of Israel's worship, here in 6:7–7:7 it is her morality. It stems from the fact that like "Adam, they have broken the covenant" (Hosea 6:7). God had entered into a covenant with them at Mount Sinai, and said, "I will bless you, but you must keep my laws" (see Exodus 19:5–6). But the people weren't living in relationship with God. They didn't care about His commands. They just did what was right in their own eyes.

Disregard for God and His authority had led to violence (Hosea 6:8), which even the clergy were committing (6:9). It had led to both spiritual harlotry and sexual immorality (6:10) as well as dishonesty (7:1).

God says, "They do not realise that I remember all their evil deeds"

(7:2). Even if the people were never brought to justice, God saw it all. But they had forgotten God, so they had no sense of any personal obligation to Him or His laws.

The kings were no better (7:3). Verses 5–6 explain how, after Jeroboam II, king after king seized the throne by killing off his rivals. With six kings dying in the span of 30 years, it is little wonder Hosea says, "they devour their rulers. All their kings fall" (7:7). Why was this happening? The verse ends with this sad observation: "none of them calls on me"—the King of kings! The rulers weren't praying or asking God for His thoughts and directions.

From top to bottom, the people had lost their way morally, because they had rejected God.

Heavenly Father, forgive me when I disobey you and disappoint you. Help me to follow your laws with delight, and so love to please you. For Jesus' sake, amen.

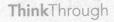

Can you sense God's frustration in Hosea 7:1? Are there any areas of disobedience that might be preventing you from experiencing His restoration and healing?

Look at Hosea 7:7. What might stop you from calling on God, even though you need Him?

Day 14

Read Hosea 7:8–16

Perhaps the most hurtful thing about Israel's behaviour was her ingratitude towards God. Even when Assyria was mobilising its forces and absorbing all the little nations as it expanded ever closer, Israel would not turn to Him (Hosea 7:10). Instead, in her arrogance, she acted as though she were some hotshot nation herself, trying to broker a deal with the big powers of the Middle East—Egypt and Assyria.

Hosea now ridicules Israel. He likens her, first of all, to a pancake that is uncooked on one side and burnt on the other (v. 8). Her foreign policy is half-baked. Then he likens Israel to an old man who refuses to accept his age (v. 9), for thinking that she is still the great Davidic Empire and can cut it on the international stage. She should have returned to God, but her arrogance blinds her (v. 10).

So, because she is like a frantic dove (v. 11), flying to Egypt one minute and to Assyria the next (depending on who looked strongest), God will catch Israel in His net and bring her down (v. 12).

God took the offence personally. He says, "Woe to them, because they have strayed from me!" (v. 13).

He promises: "For this they will be ridiculed in the land of Egypt" (v. 16). The very nation whom Israel looked to for help will scorn her. That's how grieved God is: He would rather let His people be laughed at than bless them in their rebellion.

Yet, notice God's longing for His people in verse 13: "I long to redeem them but they speak about me falsely." He aches to hear Israel cry out to Him in repentance, but they continue to pray to their pagan idols and "turn away from [Him]" (v. 14). God had trained them and strengthened them, but all they do is "plot evil against [Him]" (v. 15).

That was Israel's response to all the goodness God had shown her. How could He remain indifferent to that?

Heavenly Father, thank you for redeeming me, strengthening me, and training me. Help me not to be arrogant and think that I can do without you today. For your name's sake, amen.

What had God done for His people Israel (v. 15)? But what is their problem (v. 14)? Why is it astonishing that God still longs to redeem them (v. 13)? What does that say about God?

Where might you be in danger of becoming arrogant? How might you be guilty of no longer crying out to God from your heart? What is your response to God's goodness to you? What should you do?

Read Hosea 8:1–10

Chapter 8 begins with a warning: "Put the trumpet to your lips!" (Hosea 8:1). For "an eagle" (the Hebrew word can also mean "a vulture") is about to swoop down and destroy Israel. Why? God explains: "because the people have broken my covenant and rebelled against my law" (v. 1). Israel was throwing away the covenant that bound God to His people, and Hosea knew from his own broken marriage how God felt about that kind of abandonment. In previous chapters, he described the pain, disappointment, and frustration God has borne.

Now, we begin to feel God's anger: "My anger burns against them. How long will they be incapable of purity? They are from Israel!" (vv. 5–6). It beggars belief that God's people—so loved, so blessed—could have treated their relationship with Him with such contempt.

Israel's contempt for God showed in her self-reliance (vv. 4–10). She appointed kings without asking God what He thought (v. 4). The people were happy to let might be right; they never considered that God's support was necessary for any government to prosper.

They also created their own state religion (vv. 5–6). Hosea has spoken much about their worship of Baal, but here he highlights how they were worshipping the two golden calves that were first set up by King Jeroboam I (see 1 Kings 12:27–30) instead of God.

Israel even sold herself like a prostitute to the nation that could offer her the best pact (Hosea 8:8–9). So God was going to give her over to the "mighty king" of Assyria (v.10), and her fortified cities would be ruined (v. 14). She would reap what she had sown (v. 7).

Self-reliance makes God angry. If you see any trace of this in you, it would be good to turn from it now and to put your total trust in Him.

Heavenly Father, help me to love you so much that I refuse to rely on myself. May I actively trust you in all things. In Jesus' name, amen.

What is Israel likened to in verse 9? Why? How is this reminiscent of Hosea 4:16 and 6:4? How might you be like Israel? How does God feel about that?

Have you reached a stage in life where you believe in Jesus Christ, but you don't need Him or rely on Him, and rely on yourself instead?

What about your church? Have you come to rely more on gifted members, money, nice buildings, or good preaching, but not on God?

Day 16

Read Hosea 8:11–14

The eagle, or vulture, circles above the house of Israel (Hosea 8:1). Why? It wasn't because the places of worship were empty. No. "Israel cries out to me, 'Our God, we acknowledge you!'" (v. 2). This may have been a line from one of the temple liturgies, or perhaps an impromptu outburst from a member in the congregation. Either way, it sounded spiritual enough.

It wasn't that sacrifices weren't being offered at the altar, either. "Ephraim built many altars for sin offerings" (v. 11), and "They offer sacrifices as gifts to me, and though they eat the meat" (v. 13). They were obeying God's sacrificial laws as given in Leviticus 1–8 and 16.

Why, then, was the vulture eyeing its prey? Surely these were signs of life, not decay. Well, look at verses 2–3: "Israel cries out to me, 'Our God, we acknowledge you!' *But Israel has rejected what is good.*" Verse 11, too, says: "Though Ephraim built many altars for sin offerings, *these have become altars for sinning.*" And let the words of verse 13 sink in: "They offer sacrifices as gifts to me, and though they eat the meat, *the LORD is not pleased with them. Now he will remember their wickedness and punish their sins.*"

The people said the words, "Our God, we acknowledge you", but there was no goodness in them. They brought their sin offerings but there was no real change in their moral behaviour. They had given up obeying the Ten Commandments long ago (v. 12). It was all religious window-dressing, and God would pass judgement on it. He would send them back to the place where He had found them: Egypt, where they had once lived as slaves (v. 13).

God hates religious hypocrisy. So does Jesus. To the Pharisees of His day, He said: "Woe to you . . . you hypocrites! You clean the outside of the cup and dish, but inside they are full of greed and self-indulgence" (Matthew 23:25). John the Baptist put his finger on it. He says, "Produce fruit in keeping with repentance. And do not begin to say to yourselves, 'We have Abraham as our father'" (Luke 3:8).

Genuine repentance is what God looks for. Not your words, but your life; not your singing on Sunday, but your obedience on Monday through Saturday. So pray for His grace, that you might be real on the inside as well as the outside.

Heavenly Father, help me to be genuine. May I not simply praise you with my lips, but also by leading an obedient life. In Jesus' name, amen.

How does Hosea
8:14 remind you
of 2:13?

Read the strong
words of Jesus
against religious
hypocrisy in Matthew
23:23–28. How does
Jesus feel about it?
Spend some time
praying against any
form of religious
hypocrisy in your life.

Read Hosea 9:1–6

Christians have the greatest news in the world. God, in His great love and rich mercy, has forgiven us and drawn us to himself through His Son Jesus Christ. No wonder Paul exhorts believers to "rejoice in the Lord always!" (Philippians 4:4).

However, there are times when celebrating is the last thing God wants us to do. Hosea begins chapter 9 with such a message: "Do not rejoice, Israel; do not be jubilant like the other nations" (v. 1). Perhaps the Israelites are preparing to celebrate the Feast of Tabernacles (one of their harvest festivals), and just as they're about to tuck into their food, Hosea shouts out, "All the other nations can celebrate, but not you, Israel!"

Why would God say that? Verse 1 tells us: "For you have been unfaithful to your God; you love the wages of a prostitute at every threshing floor." The people had compromised their true faith and turned to false religion. They'd been worshipping the pagan god Baal by getting involved in ritualised sex on the threshing floors during harvest. They paid money to Baal prostitutes and performed the ritual in the hope of getting a bumper crop.

At the same time, the people were still going to God's temple and offering sacrifices to the Lord. They were trying to hedge their bets, thinking they could worship both deities at the same time.

No wonder God tells the people not to come near Him with their joyful songs in worship! Their actions were empty. He would make all their harvests poor (vv. 2–3), and He would evict them from the land. They'd go back to being slaves (as they had been in Egypt), but this time in Assyria, where it would be hard to celebrate (v. 4). In fact, when the feast days came round, they would still gather—but not for celebrations. Instead, it would be for mass burials (vv. 5–6). God promises that the land that was once fertile will soon become a wilderness (v. 6).

God is rightly jealous. As the Creator of the universe, He alone is worthy of praise. To agree with the popular view that all religions are the same might make for an easier life, but it is a compromise. It grieves God and He will say to us, "Do not rejoice!"

Heavenly Father, you are the one true God, so help me to worship you alone. In Jesus' name, amen.

On what note
does the chapter
begin? Why is this
surprising?

How does God feel
about the people's
compromise? What
does that tell you
about Him? What
response should that
evoke in us?

Day 18

Read Hosea 9:7–9

We read at the beginning of chapter 9 that there were times when God did not want His people to rejoice. Israel's worship of Baal meant that they were "two-timing" Him. Their songs of praise to Him were empty. But God was sickened not only by their compromised worship; verses 7–9 show us another reason why God insists they should not rejoice.

God was appalled by the way the people treated His prophet and His Word. Hosea's marriage to Gomer the prostitute was meant to be a sermon to the nation. Just as Hosea continued to love his unfaithful wife, so God continued to love His unfaithful people. But the nation didn't like it. They considered Hosea a fool, and sought to trip him up. And it was the religious leaders who gave him the hardest time of all (Hosea 9:7–8).

This shouldn't surprise us, of course. **We far prefer to hear words that pat us on the back than those that sting.** The problem with Hosea is that he keeps reminding the people of their numerous sins (v. 7). He even goes so far as to compare their present corruption with one of their most shameful past episodes: "They have sunk deep into corruption, as in the days of Gibeah" (v. 9).

In Judges 19, a Levite's concubine was brutally raped and murdered by some bisexual men of Gibeah. "Such a thing has never been seen or done, not since the day the Israelites came up out of Egypt" (Judges 19:30). But Hosea now says that Israel's sin is far worse! As if that isn't enough, the prophet speaks of their ultimate doom: "the days of reckoning are at hand" (Hosea 9:7).

God had sent Hosea to be a watchman (v. 8). The watchman's job was to stand on the walls, and to sound the alarm to warn the nation when he saw disaster approaching. That's what Hosea was doing, but the people would rather have someone sing them a soothing lullaby. Tragically, they didn't want to hear the Word that could have saved them.

So, God insists that as long as they refuse to listen to His words of warning, they should not rejoice.

Lord God, thank you for loving me enough to warn me. Help me to humble myself and to take your Word to heart, even when it stings, because you meant for it not to harm me but to make me more like Jesus. In His Name, amen.

What is "at hand" in verse 7? What is Hosea to do with that knowledge? Notice where he faced the greatest danger. What does that tell you? How would you apply that today?

Why is opposition to God's Word so terrible? Why do we need to hear the hard words, and not just the comforting ones?

Day 19

Read Hosea 9:10–17

God is looking back, remembering the days when He first found Israel. You can almost hear His delight and tenderness: "When I found Israel, it was like finding grapes in the desert" (Hosea 9:10). Then the grim reality: "But when they came to Baal Peor, they consecrated themselves to that shameful idol and became as vile as the thing they loved."

Numbers 25 relates the story of how the Israelite soldiers were enticed by Moabite women into having sex at the local Baal shrine. First love quickly evaporated, and the grapes turned sour. And now, in Hosea's day, it was happening all over again.

No wonder God's patience has run out. Time and again He had forgiven Israel and warned her, but still she persisted in her unfaithfulness. Now, terrible punishment is due. Her glory (God himself) will fly away ("when I turn away from them", v. 12), she will become infertile (ironic, because Baal was supposed to be a fertility god), and war will come to her (vv. 12–13), which will again lead to the death of her children.

As Hosea realises the horror of what God has in store for Israel, he tries to pray (v. 14). He knows that things have gone too far and that sin must be punished, but he longs for Israel's punishment to be softened. So he prays for her children to never come into existence, so they wouldn't have to suffer such a horrid future.

God's passion is revealed in verses 15–17. Gilgal, the centre of Baal worship, represented the two-timing attitude of the nation, and God hated it. Of Israel, He now says, "I will no longer love them" (v. 15), and they will become "wanderers among the nations" (v. 17). They would still be His people but, for a while, God was going to have to use shock treatment and withdraw His affection.

Let these red hot words sink deep into your heart. **When God loves, He loves with intensity and for keeps.** Like Israel, we can offend, grieve, and disappoint Him. If we abandon Him as our first love and continue to cheat on Him, God will say to us: "Do not rejoice!" (v. 1).

Heavenly Father, thank you for your passionate love towards me. Help me never to take that love for granted, and may you always be my first love. In Jesus' name, amen.

How does God feel
at the beginning of
verse 10? What does
that tell you about
Him?

Turn to Revelation
2:4–5. What had the
church in Ephesus
done? What would
Jesus do if they did
not repent? What
important lessons
can you learn
from this?

Day 20

Read Hosea 10:1–8

Some people think of God as a kind, grandfather-like figure who would never do anyone any harm. He's there to smile on us and pat us on the back. The Bible, however, gives us a very different picture. In it we discover a God who is utterly good and who burns with love, but who is passionately committed to eradicating evil and who cares enough to act. We are frequently told to fear Him.

When the holy God shows up, it's terrifying. Rather than face Him, people cry out to the mountains, "Cover us!", and to the hills, "Fall on us!" (Hosea 10:8). I wonder if we need to learn from this. Have we so domesticated our idea of God that we can't imagine ever needing to "fear Him"? If so, Hosea is showing us a side to God that we must never forget.

Three things led to God's judgement on His people. The first was their wealth. Like a flourishing vine, the nation had prospered (v. 1) and become fruitful, but with money came idolatry and a "deceitful"—or, literally, "divided"—heart (v. 2). Money can do that to you: you may think you can buy anything, even God. You can't.

The second was Israel's leadership. The people swung between two extremes. In their arrogance, they thought they could get rid of their rulers and it didn't matter what God thought (v. 3). In their apathy, they thought none of their leaders could be trusted (v. 4). Either way, the people had no respect for their God-appointed leaders.

The third was their worship. Beth Aven ("house of wickedness", v. 5), or Bethel, was where Jeroboam I had set up the calf-idol as the centre of Israel's national religion. It had institutionalised idolatry and beguiled the people. Hosea called the religious leaders what they were—"idolatrous priests" (v. 5). Instead of helping the nation to turn back to God, Bethel was adding to the people's guilt and plunging them more deeply into sin.

Israel would lose everything: her calf-idol (v. 5), her affluence (vv. 6, 8), and her leaders (v. 7). She would learn that it is a terrifying thing to fall into the hands of the living God (v. 8).

Almighty and most merciful Father, teach me to fear you above anything and everything else, that I might gain a heart of wisdom. For Jesus' sake, amen.

Look up Mark 10:17–31 and Revelation 3:17–19. How can prosperity lead to our spiritual downfall?

How can you make sure you have a godly attitude towards those who lead you (including work, church, and national leaders)?

When can a church do more harm than good?

Day 21

Read Hosea 10:9–15

It could all have been so different. You hear the sad story of someone who took a wrong turn in life, or of someone who made bad choices, and you can't help wondering if things could have turned out better if that step hadn't been taken or that door had remained closed.

It could all have been so different for Israel too. Terrible judgement was on its way because she had refused to learn from her past. Once more (see Hosea 9:9) Hosea refers to the terrible incident at Gibeah (Hosea 10:9), recorded in Judges 19. It had involved homosexual lust, gang rape, and murder, and ended with Israel sending an army to sort it out. Thousands had died.

Now that the same things were happening again, God would have to send the army in once more. This time, however, it would come from the surrounding nations (v. 10), who would put Israel in chains.

The trouble was that Israel had simply "remained" in her sins (v. 9) and not turned from them.

What's more, she had wasted so many opportunities. God had spotted Ephraim (another name for Israel) like a farmer spots a young cow, and He has decided to harness it (vv. 11–12). He had given His people chance after chance to sow seeds of righteousness and reap the harvest of His covenant love, but they had thrown it all away. "But you have planted wickedness" (v. 13), says God.

Instead of seeking the Lord, who stood ready to bless Israel, she had depended on her "own strength" and on her "many warriors" (v. 13). Now, God would show her just how foolish she was to trust in military might and not in Him. He would destroy all her fortresses (v. 14) and it would be "because [her] wickedness is great" (v. 15). **In God's eyes, it is always better to be right than to be strong.**

It could all have been so different. Don't make the same mistakes that Israel made. Hosea cries out, "it is time to seek the LORD" (v. 12). Listen to that heartfelt cry and learn from it.

Heavenly Father, thank you for inviting me to seek after you. Thank you that in Jesus, I may truly know you and be blessed. Help me to depend on you today. For your name's sake, amen.

How does Revelation 6:12–17 pick up on the imagery of Hosea 10:8? What terrible and terrifying scene does John depict here?

Why do we need to read Hosea 10 and Revelation 6? How does this help us to understand God, and what the world is coming to?

Day 22

Read Hosea 11:1–4

We've reached one of the most poignant scenes in the whole of the Bible. Hosea shows us God alone, talking to himself. As we hear the agonising thoughts and feelings of God, we begin to see Him as a broken-hearted Father, grieving over His wayward child, Israel. It is a vivid, tenderly drawn picture.

Look at verse 1: "When Israel was a child, I loved him, and out of Egypt I called my son." God is reminiscing, not for the first time (see Hosea 9:10; 10:1). Like a man who finds an orphaned baby, buys him out of slavery, adopts him, and calls him "my son", God has done the same with Israel.

He remembers how He has lovingly nursed His infant son, helped him to take his first faltering steps, and applied cream to his bumps and bruises (Hosea 11:3). The New English Bible translates verse 4 like this: "I harnessed them in leading strings and led them with bonds of love—that I lifted them like a little child to my cheek, that I had bent down to feed them." It's a beautiful picture. Here is the Almighty God of the universe bending down to choose a people, love them, train them, and care for them. Here is a generous, gentle, devoted Father.

With such parenting, you would have thought that this child would have turned out brilliantly, wouldn't you? But listen in and discover the sad truth: "they did not realise it was I who healed them" (v. 3). God is saying: "They don't appreciate it. The more I call their name, the further they go away from me and settle in the arms of other gods" (v. 2, paraphrased).

Perhaps you know the pain of rejected love. You can be the most considerate, patient, loving parent, spouse or child, and still your loved one turns against you. Hosea knew that. Can you believe that God knows how that feels too?

We also learn here just how awful sin is. We tend to think of it as an impersonal breach of the rules, but that's wrong. **To sin is to turn your back on the God who loves you. It is to hurt and grieve Him.**

Almighty God, thank you for being my Heavenly Father. Thank you for your great love to me. Help me to love you. In the name of Christ, amen.

Review verses 1–4
and think about how
God is your heavenly
Father, in Christ. Is
this how you view
Him? Thank Him for
His love.

How helpful is it
to see sin in such
personal terms—"sin
is to turn your back
on the God who
loves you"?

How does Hosea
anticipate Jesus
in verse 1? (see
Matthew 2:13–18.)

Day 23

Read Hosea 11:5–7

The mood quickly changes. This gentle, tender Father now becomes furious at His son's repeated rejection: "Will they not return to Egypt and will not Assyria rule over them because they refuse to repent? A sword will flash in their cities; it will devour their false prophets and put an end to their plans" (Hosea 11:5–6).

God had lavished His love on Israel, but all He got in return was the cold shoulder. It was time she learned how that felt. He had found her in Egypt, and if she didn't want Him, He would send her back there. She didn't want His love, so He would let her feel the sword instead.

The problem was deep-rooted: "My people are determined to turn from me" (v. 7). Now God would not come running when Israel called out to Him in her trouble. It was time for Him to withdraw and to let her realise just where her choices would lead her. "Even though they call me God Most High, I will by no means exalt them" (v. 7).

These are no empty words. God's anger is real, and in just a few years (722 BC), Israel would be invaded by Assyria and the people carted off into slavery.

God is a devoted Father, but that does not mean He is a pushover. In the end, He will punish all who spurn His generous love.

We see that there is a legitimate place for anger. For example, when people are abused and ill treated, we ought to be furious. However, in our anger we must not sin (Psalm 4:4); neither should we greet injustice with disinterest.

We must take God's anger seriously too. God loved Israel, but that didn't stop Him from sending Assyria to discipline her. God loves the whole world, but He still warns us of hell. Anger isn't the opposite of love; it actually arises from it. God generously offers to make us His children, just as He did with Israel, but if we continually rebuff and scorn His love, He will not simply shrug His shoulders and move on. He will be angry.

Heavenly Father, I thank you for caring enough about me and your world to get angry when we reject you. Help me to never spurn your love. In Jesus' name, amen.

Can you think of a situation where it is right to get angry? How do we ensure that in our anger we do not sin?

Why is it good that God gets angry? How is His anger different from ours?

Day 24

Read Hosea 11:8–11

God was so deeply hurt by Israel's spiritual adultery that He said He would send His people into exile (Hosea 11:6). Yet, in the very next breath, He says, "How can I give you up, Ephraim? How can I hand you over, Israel? How can I treat you like Admah? How can I make you like Zeboyim? My heart is changed within me; all my compassion is aroused" (v. 8). Again, we see God agonising over His people, like a father wrestling over the wayward child He loves.

Admah and Zeboyim were two of the cities God completely destroyed when He judged Sodom and Gomorrah (Deuteronomy 29:23). That's how strongly God feels about His people playing fast and loose with Him. But He also insists: "I will not carry out my fierce anger" (Hosea 11:9).

As we listen in on God, we see the conundrum at the very heart of His character. On the one hand, God cannot deny His justice, for He is just. On the other, He cannot deny His mercy, for God is love. And if He were to do either of these and not the other, He would be less than God.

Humanly speaking, there is no way out of this. That's why God says, "For I am God, and not a man—the Holy One among you. I will not come in wrath" (v. 9). The Roman poet Horace famously told his academy of poets: "Never bring a god upon the stage unless your problem is such that it demands a god to resolve it." If God was going to be just and loving towards His people, God himself would resolve it.

Assyria will invade and God will be just (v. 10), but unlike Admah and Zeboyim, Israel will survive and one day, God will summon those He has scattered and bring them home. How can God do that? By personally intervening upon the human stage and, out of love, taking the full blow that His justice demands in our place.

Hosea anticipates Jesus' sacrifice. **It is only at the cross that we find that God is both love and utterly just, and neither is compromised.** The anger that we deserved for betraying Him, Christ suffered on our behalf, and all that remains is His love for us.

Heavenly Father, thank you so much for Jesus. Thank you for the cross, where wrath and mercy meet. Amen.

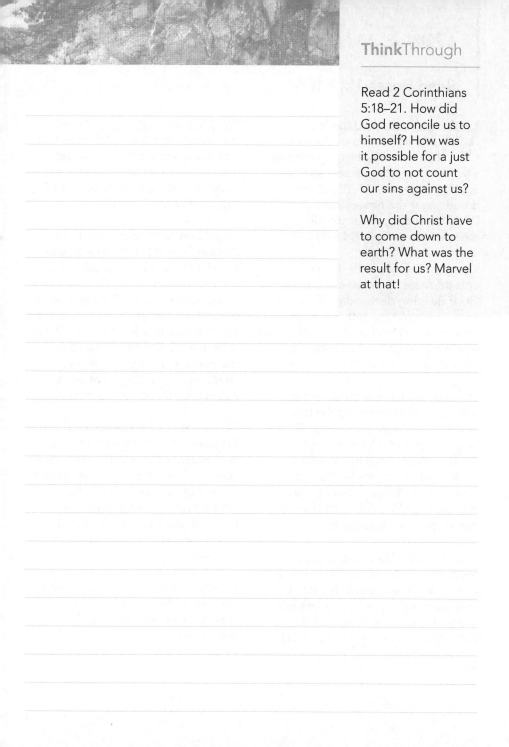

Read 2 Corinthians 5:18–21. How did God reconcile us to himself? How was it possible for a just God to not count our sins against us?

Why did Christ have to come down to earth? What was the result for us? Marvel at that!

Read Hosea 11:12–12:6

We've reached the final four chapters of Hosea's prophecy which reiterate the themes of the book: Israel's spiritual adultery (Hosea 11:12–12:14), the divine anger she has aroused (13:1–16), and God's longing for a renewed relationship (14:1–9).

Chapter 12 begins with Israel's unfaithfulness. How has she offended God? By living deceitfully: "Ephraim has surrounded me with lies, Israel with deceit" (11:12). Judah (in the south) is little better, but Israel has tried to live a double life.

She sought to follow the Lord, but she continued to worship the pagan deities too. She was unfaithful. Notice how, by contrast, Hosea refers to the one whom Israel has sought to deceive. He is "the faithful Holy One" (11:12). **What God says, He does. When He makes a promise, He keeps it.**

Israel's double life was also seen in her foreign policy. On the one hand, she tried to keep Assyria happy by making a treaty with her. On the other, she sent olive oil to Egypt in tribute (12:1). She should have fed on God's Word (Deuteronomy 8:3), but instead she "feeds on the wind" (Hosea 12:1), whichever way she thought it was blowing. She was deceitful at every level. Ultimately, it will all be futile (like eating wind!).

Hosea now turns to include Judah in his indictment. In many ways she was like her forefather Jacob, who grasped his older brother's heel (12:3) and pretended to be Esau in order to snatch his inheritance. Yet God turned that "grasping" into a blessing. It was at Bethel (12:4, notice Hosea uses its real name instead of the nickname "Beth Aven" this time) that Jacob was humbled and transformed.

God holds out the possibility of doing the same again (12:6) with Jacob's descendants. If she would only learn from her forefather and return to Him instead of to a golden calf, she too would have a future. It was, after all, the Lord who had brought about the reversal in Jacob's fortunes, and no one else.

Heavenly Father, you can turn Jacob into Israel. Please perform that change in me too. For Jesus' sake, amen.

In what ways might you be living a double life? What motivations do these verses give you to shun that way of living?

How did God take the "grasping" nature of Jacob and change that around for good? What can we learn from Jacob's example?

Day 26

Read Hosea 12:7–14

Hosea is shining the spotlight on Israel's double life—her infidelity that has so grieved God. Her pretence at devotion to Yahweh (while worshipping other gods) and her duplicity in foreign affairs (courting Egypt while flirting with Assyria) were not her only crimes (Hosea 12:7–9).

The sad truth is that God's child, Israel, has turned out to be just like all the other kids.

Israel has become like "the merchant" (literally "Canaanite") who "uses dishonest scales" and "loves to defraud" (v. 7). God had brought the Israelites out of Egypt (v. 9) and had given them the land that was occupied by the wicked Canaanites. He had said to Israel, "Do not defile yourselves in any of these ways, because this is how the nations that I am going to drive out before you became defiled. Even the land was defiled; so I punished it for its sin, and the land vomited out its inhabitants" (Leviticus 18:24–25). Israel was supposed to have been a distinct, different, and holy nation (see Exodus 19:6). Instead, she had simply copied all the dishonest practices of the peoples around her. She had become like the world.

Israel's dishonesty had made her wealthy (Hosea 12:8), and her riches had made her arrogant and blind. It's a well-worn path. Years later, the Laodiceans went the same way (see Revelation 3:17–19), and the result was a church that the Lord Jesus found repulsive.

Israel's sins made God feel the same way. She provoked His anger (Hosea 12:14). If the only way He could shock her into repentance was to evict her from the land and make her into a homeless people once again, He would do it. Her religiosity (v. 11) would not save her. If she thought she could devise her own clever schemes, like her father Jacob, and that she no longer needed God (v. 12), she would have another thing coming.

It could all have been so different, if Israel had only listened to the prophets God had sent to her through the years to warn her, to rescue her, and to care for her (vv. 10, 13). But God's people had ignored His Word and gone their own merry way. They would now pay for their sins (v. 14).

Heavenly Father, help me to be wholly yours, holy and distinct. For Jesus' sake, amen.

Read Deuteronomy 28:9–11. What was supposed to happen? But what had happened instead by Hosea's day (Hosea 12:7)?

In what ways could you become like the world around you? Where are the dangers? What does Christ want you to become instead (see Matthew 5:13–16)?

Read Hosea 13:1–3

With this penultimate chapter comes the darkest part of Hosea's prophecy. God gives full vent to His fierce anger against His unchaste bride. But it also comes as God looks back on Israel's past once more.

In just a few sentences (Hosea 13:1–3) Hosea sketches Israel's demise. He moves swiftly from the past (v. 1) to the present (v. 2), and then the future (v. 3). There was a time when Ephraim (the dominant tribe in the north) spoke and all the other tribes and surrounding nations sat up and listened. But Hosea quickly traces the moment when Israel sowed the seeds of her own downfall back to when the people turned from Yahweh (the source of life and strength) to worshipping Baal (v. 1). At that point, even though they continued to exist, it was as if their relationship with God had died (and the people with it).

Stepping away from the living God and towards idolatry, they had started something that they couldn't control. Their flirtation with sin became addictive and gave birth to more and more sin (v. 2). Now they found themselves in the ridiculous situation of getting their highly skilled craftsman to make cows for people to kiss. It would be laughable if it wasn't so tragic.

God promises that in the future, this once-great kingdom would go up in smoke (v. 3). Like the morning mist or the dew that quickly evaporates, and like the husk around the wheat that is blown away by the wind, Israel would disappear.

And she did. All too soon the "east wind" (v. 15) of the Assyrian military machine blew in and took everything, including people and goods (the capital city of Samaria was known for its affluence). Even their next generation was removed as soldiers slaughtered little ones and pregnant women (v. 16).

All this would happen because the people had "rebelled against their God" and "must bear their guilt" (v. 16). Israel fell not because she was poor, nor because Assyria was stronger, but because she had abandoned the Lord and chased after Baal. **Walking away from God only brings our own demise.**

Heavenly Father, thank you for being the source of life, love, strength, and goodness. Help me to love you and not flirt with anyone or anything that might threaten my devotion to you. In Jesus' name, amen.

As Hosea looks back at Israel's past (v. 1), what does he remember? How does he describe what had happened to them?

What is the present result (v. 2)? How does sin trap us and spiral out of control?

So what will God do now (vv. 3, 15–16)? What does this tell us about God?

Day 28

Read Hosea 13:4–12

What arouses God's anger? We've seen Israel's unfaithfulness and how she went after Baal and the calf-idols (Hosea 13:1–3); that certainly did it. But it isn't just idolatry. Pride provokes God's anger too.

God had heard Israel's cries in Egypt (v. 4) and saved her. The people had stood at Mount Sinai and heard God say, "You shall have no other gods before me" (see Exodus 20:3). They had been showered with gifts as He provided for them and met their every need (Hosea 13:5). No other nation has known the privileges that Israel had.

But the more God gave her, the more highly she thought of herself and her own abilities. She quickly forgot God (v. 6) and thought she didn't need Him. This pride and ingratitude made God furious. He may have been like a father or a husband, but Israel would soon see Him in a very different guise. He would turn on her like some ferocious predator—like a lion, a leopard, or a bear (vv. 7–8).

Idolatry, pride, and one other thing all kindle God's wrath—unbelief. Israel would be destroyed because instead of trusting God, her "helper" (v. 9), she wanted a king to believe in.

God had allowed the nation to have a king in His law (see Deuteronomy 17:14–20), but they wanted one for all the wrong reasons. You can read the sorry tale in 1 Samuel 8. They wanted a military leader who could secure their future, "a king to lead us, such as all the other nations have" (1 Samuel 8:5). God saw it for what it was: "they have rejected me as their king" (1 Samuel 8:7). He gave them what they asked for, but where had it got them? Their monarch had become little more than a puppet of the Assyrian empire! If only they had not looked to their rulers, but to the Lord God (Hosea 13:4).

God had been so patient, but Israel's record of continued idolatry, pride, and unbelief could not be ignored (v. 12). In the end, God's anger would burn against her, and she would feel it.

Heavenly Father, thank you for being far more patient than I could ever be, and may I never take that patience for granted. Help me to run from sin. For Jesus' sake, amen.

Hosea 13:4 quotes Exodus 20:2–3. What does God say in Exodus 20:4? How is God described and what does that tell us about Him?

Read 1 Samuel 8:4–18 where Israel asks for a king. What do we learn about God and about ourselves from this story?

Day 29

Read Hosea 13:13–16

Just when we think that Israel's sin is so great and God so furious that the nation's end is certain, Hosea surprises us. In the final words of this chapter, hope begins to flicker once more.

Hosea cries, "Pains as of a woman in childbirth come to him" (Hosea 13:13). The suffering that Israel is about to endure from the Assyrian invasion need not be her death throes; they could be the pains of childbirth! The situation before God's people doesn't have to be terminal; life could still be snatched from the jaws of death. The only trouble is Israel's stubbornness: "he is a child without wisdom; when the time arrives, he doesn't have the sense to come out of the womb" (v. 13).

So, because Israel chooses the grave instead of being reborn, God says: "I will have no compassion . . . An east wind from the LORD will come, blowing in from the desert . . . They will fall by the sword; their little ones will be dashed to the ground, their pregnant women ripped open" (vv. 14–16). If only Israel would choose life and repent; instead, her stubborn refusal means this will be her last chance.

Yet, even though this generation chooses death, God will not give up on His people: "I will deliver this people from the power of the grave; I will redeem them from death" (v. 14). Israel might be faithless, but God had committed himself to her at Mount Sinai (v. 4). And when He makes a promise, He keeps it, no matter what.

The apostle Paul knew this. As he writes about God's ultimate triumph over our greatest enemies of sin, death, and hell, it is with these words that he concludes: "When the perishable has been clothed with the imperishable, and the mortal with immortality, then the saying that is written will come true: 'Death has been swallowed up in victory.' 'Where, O death, is your victory? Where, O death, is your sting?'" (1 Corinthians 15:54–55).

Hosea knew in a deep and personal way that God's love for His people never gives up. Death and hell might seem to threaten it, but it is invincible. That is the grace of God, and therein lies our hope.

Heavenly Father, thank you for your love that never gives up and is unconquerable. In Jesus' name, amen.

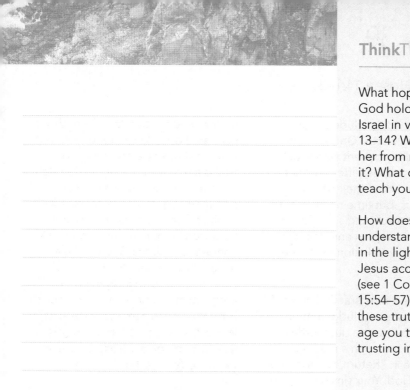

What hope does God hold out to Israel in verses 13–14? What stops her from receiving it? What does that teach you?

How does Paul understand verse 14 in the light of what Jesus accomplished (see 1 Corinthians 15:54–57)? How do these truths encourage you to keep trusting in God?

Day 30

Read Hosea 14:1–3

Chapter 13 concluded with chilling words. God had been incredibly patient with Israel. He had sent prophet after prophet to warn them about their persistent unfaithfulness, but time had run out, and He had to act. And so in 722 BC, the Assyrians swept in and destroyed Samaria, the capital, along with the rest of the kingdom.

Is God finished with Israel? Chapter 14 provides the answer. Judgement has fallen, and now, as the dust settles, God sends Hosea with a message. Look at verse 1: "Return, Israel, to the LORD your God. Your sins have been your downfall!"

Notice how Hosea calls God "your God". It's an astonishing invitation! Despite everything, God will still have Israel back. In fact, He is waiting for them to return. They will have to come not with empty sacrifices (as they had done in the temple for so many years), but with serious words of apology (Hosea 14:2), genuine repentance (v. 3), and with a determination to walk away from their past ("We will never again") and from thinking they can save themselves ("what our own hands have made").

And what will they find when they return to Him? A Father of compassion (v. 3) who longs to take care of those in need. I don't know about you, but I find that utterly astonishing. The words at the end of chapter 13 might have sent a shiver down our spine— and they ought to have, for rebellion against God is utterly serious and God won't ignore it. But chapter 14 contains the words God far prefers to say; this is where His heart lies. Even after passing judgement, He longs for His people to come back to Him. **Like the father looking, waiting, and aching for his son's homecoming, so God yearns for us to return.**

It says something about human pride and stubbornness that it took a national disaster to bring the people of Israel to the point where they would sincerely pray like this, doesn't it? How much tragedy might God have to allow into your life before you're willing to approach Him with similar words of humility, honesty, and genuine sorrow?

Gracious Father, thank you that in spite of all my sin, you long for me to be with you. Help me to remember that. For Jesus' sake, amen.

Why is the appeal of Hosea 14:1 such a surprise after 13:14–16?

What does God long for? How does Hosea describe God in verses 1 and 3? Why is that so astonishing and so encouraging?

Day 31

Read Hosea 14:4–9

We've reached the end of our love story. Was Hosea's marriage to Gomer ever fully restored? The prophet doesn't tell us. What we do know is that the greater love story that Hosea's marriage was supposed to reflect still goes on, for the God of Israel is the God and Father of the Lord Jesus, and He is determined to have a people for himself, whatever they've done.

Listen to His appeal: "Return, Israel, to the LORD your God" (Hosea 14:1), and hear His promise to those who come: "I will heal their waywardness and love them freely, for my anger has turned away from them" (v. 4). God is determined to love His people and if they're incapable of remaining faithful, His strength will supply their weakness. He "will heal their waywardness".

God's love will be the key to Israel finding new life. Like the dew, it will refresh them and enable them to blossom (v. 5). The nation, now broken, will once again stand tall (v. 6) and will prosper (v. 7) under God's care: "your fruitfulness comes from me" (v. 8).

However, after the Assyrian invasion, Israel was no more. Judah survived for a bit longer, but was later conquered by the Babylonians. Eventually, some survivors came back and resettled, but the nation was a shadow of what it had once been. Yet, the faithful clung to verses like these, believing that God's promises would come true one day.

And they did. In Jesus, God himself burst onto the scene and promised life in all its fullness for Israel and Judah, for Jew and Gentile. Life would come, but only as Jesus embraced death and turned the anger of God away from us. Three days later, when Jesus shattered the barrier of death and rose from the dead, He proved that nothing is as unconquerable as God's love. When He promises, "[I will] love them freely" (v. 4), He means it, whatever the cost.

Hosea ends with a postscript in verse 9. He doesn't want any of his words to go to waste. Therefore, be wise before God and be determined to act on what you've learned.

Heavenly Father, thank you for all that Hosea has taught me about your persistent, all-conquering, "never giving up" love. I know that love was costly. Help me to love you truly. For Jesus' sake, amen.

What will God's love do? What are the images used in verses 4 to 8? What does each image convey?

Why do you think Hosea finishes with the postscript of verse 9?

Think back over the book of Hosea. What has God shown you about himself? What do you need to remember?

Going Deeper in Your Walk with Christ

Whether you're a new Christian or have been a Christian for a while, it's worth taking a journey through the gospels of Matthew, Mark, Luke, and John. Each gospel presents a distinct aspect of Christ and helps us gain a deeper appreciation of who Jesus is, why He came, and what it means for us.

Hear His words. Witness His works. Deepen your walk with Jesus as you follow Him through the wonderful scenes painted in the gospels.

Journey Through

Matthew

The first book of the New Testament makes it abundantly clear who Jesus is: the Immanuel (God with us), and Saviour of the world. It shows us how Jesus fulfilled all that was predicted of the Messiah, and how His death and resurrection would bring salvation and reconcile people to God. Embark on a journey of the gospel of Matthew with Mike Raiter, and let this truth of Jesus' eternal authority change your walk with God. Be challenged as you take up Jesus' call to follow Him, and discover what it means to lead a life of total commitment to the Messiah.

Mike Raiter is a preacher, preaching trainer, and a former Principal of the Melbourne School of Theology in Australia. He is now the Director of Centre for Biblical Preaching and the author of a number of books, including *Stirrings of the Soul*, which won the 2004 Australian Christian Book of the year award.

Journey Through

Mark

Take time to go through the shortest gospel in the Bible, and you'll find it packs punch. Mark's gospel presents to us the living Christ and tells us who Jesus is, what He said, and what He did. It portrays Jesus as a man of action as well as words, and reminds us how we are to love God's people in practical, compassionate ways. Dig deeper into the book with Robert Solomon, and be amazed by what the Servant King has done for you. Follow in Jesus' footsteps, learn from His life on earth, and be led to a personal encounter with Him, so that you may become more and more like the Servant King.

Robert M. Solomon served as Bishop of The Methodist Church in Singapore from 2000–2012. He has an active itinerant preaching and teaching ministry in Singapore and abroad. He is the author of more than 30 books, including *The Race*, *The Conscience*, *The Sermon of Jesus*, *Faithful to the End*, *Finding Rest for the Soul*, and *God in Pursuit*.

Journey Through
Luke

From Mary's opening song to God her Saviour, to Jesus' last words to His disciples to preach repentance for the forgiveness of sins, the gospel of Luke is a proclamation of salvation. This salvation is for those to whom Jesus calls: the sick, the lost, the outcasts, and the broken.

How do we receive this salvation? By responding to Jesus' call: "Follow Me." But what does it mean to follow Jesus? And what will it cost us? Join the 12 disciples on their journey with Jesus and explore Luke's account of what they learn as they accompany their master on His long journey to Jerusalem—and to the cross. Find out what discipleship really means as you discover the joy of following Jesus.

Mike Raiter is a preacher, preaching trainer, and a former Principal of the Melbourne School of Theology in Australia. He is now the Director of Centre for Biblical Preaching and the author of a number of books, including *Stirrings of the Soul*, which won the 2004 Australian Christian Book of the year award.

Journey Through

John

The gospel of John begins with a bold declaration: "In the beginning was the Word, and the Word was with God". It then poetically introduces Jesus Christ as God incarnate—not just God himself, but also the perfect, visible expression of an invisible God whom mankind could see, hear, touch, and relate to. Unsure of your faith? Dig into the gospel of John. Discover who this unique Son of God is and anchor your faith on solid ground.

David Cook was Principal of the Sydney Missionary and Bible College for 26 years. He is an accomplished writer and has authored Bible commentaries, books on the Minor Prophets, and several Bible study guides.

Journey Through

Acts

The book of Acts is one of the most exciting parts of the Bible. Jesus has just ascended to heaven, the Spirit has come to the church, and we see God at work building the church and causing the gospel message to spread through Judea, into Samaria, throughout Asia, into Europe, and finally to Rome. Embark on a daily journey through the book of Acts, and see how the Holy Spirit empowers the church to witness in ever widening circles until the gospel reaches the ends of the earth.

David Cook was Principal of the Sydney Missionary and Bible College for 26 years. He is an accomplished writer and has authored Bible commentaries, books on the Minor Prophets, and several Bible study guides.

Journey Through

Hebrews

Have you ever had second thoughts about being a Christian? Sometimes it's hard to stay committed to Jesus amid the daily onslaught of worldly wisdom, tedium, and temptation. Let the book of Hebrews remind you about the Author and Perfecter of our faith; who He is, what He did, and why it matters. Be encouraged by the unique truth of a God who became a man to die in our place and who, as our eternal High Priest, will return bringing eternal rest for those who have anchored their faith in Him.

Robert M. Solomon served as Bishop of The Methodist Church in Singapore from 2000–2012. He has an active itinerant preaching and teaching ministry in Singapore and abroad. He is the author of more than 30 books, including *The Race, The Conscience, The Sermon of Jesus, Faithful to the End, Finding Rest for the Soul,* and *God in Pursuit.*

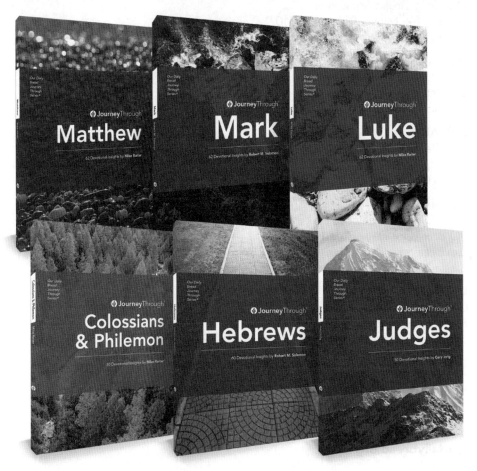

For information on our resources, visit **ourdailybread.org**. Alternatively, please contact the office nearest you from the list below, or go to **ourdailybread.org/locations** for the complete list of offices.

BELARUS
Our Daily Bread Ministries
PO Box 82, Minsk, Belarus 220107
belarus@odb.org • (375-17) 2854657; (375-29) 9168799

GERMANY
Our Daily Bread Ministries e.V.
Schulstraße 42, 79540 Lörrach
deutsch@odb.org

IRELAND
Our Daily Bread Ministries
64 Baggot Street Lower, Dublin 2, D02 XC62
ireland@odb.org • +3531 (01) 676 7315

RUSSIA
MISSION Our Daily Bread
PO Box "Our Daily Bread",
str.Vokzalnaya 2, Smolensk, Russia 214961
russia@odb.org • 8(4812)660849; +7(951)7028049

UKRAINE
Christian Mission Our Daily Bread
PO Box 533, Kiev, Ukraine 01004
ukraine@odb.org • +380964407374; +380632112446

UNITED KINGDOM (Europe Regional Office)
Our Daily Bread Ministries
PO Box 1, Carnforth, Lancashire, LA5 9ES
europe@odb.org • 015395 64149

ourdailybread.org

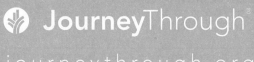

Sign up to *Journey Through*

We would love to support you with the *Journey Through* series! Please be aware we can only provide one copy of each future *Journey Through* book per reader (previous books from the series are available to purchase).

If you know of other people who would be interested in this series, we can send you introductory *Journey Through* booklets to pass onto them (which include details on how they can easily sign up for the books themselves).

☐ **I would like to regularly receive the *Journey Through* series**

☐ **Please send me ____ copies of the *Journey Through* introductory booklet**

Just complete and return this sign up form to us at:

Our Daily Bread Ministries, PO Box 1, Carnforth, Lancashire, LA5 9ES, United Kingdom

Here at Our Daily Bread Ministries we take your privacy seriously. We will only use this personal information to manage your account, and regularly provide you with *Journey Through* series books and offers of other resources, three ministry update letters each year, and occasional additional mailings with news that's relevant to you. We will also send you ministry updates and/or details of Discovery House products by email if you agree to this. In order to do this we share your details with our UK-based mailing house and Our Daily Bread Ministries in the US. We do not sell or share personal information with anyone for marketing purposes.

Please do not complete and sign this form for anyone but yourself. You do not need to complete this form if you already receive regular copies of *Journey Through* from us.

Full Name (Mr/Mrs/Miss/Ms): _____

Address: _____

_____

Postcode: _____ Tel: _____

Email: _____
☐ I would like to receive email updates and details of Discovery House products.

Signature: _____

All our resources, including *Journey Through*, are available without cost. Many people, making even the smallest of donations, enable Our Daily Bread Ministries to reach others with the life-changing wisdom of the Bible. We are not funded or endowed by any group or denomination.